These farts belong to

_____

Tinker & SWAG on Amazon

NEW RELEASES coming for Dragons and Jessie & Jamie.
For sneak peeks, special insights, and alerts, please sign up at
www.tinkerandswag.com
Meanwhile, enjoy the current selection!

How to Catch a Dragosauricorn

A topsy turvy game of chase through
Jessie & Jamie's favorite places.
What will they learn when the game is over?

Into the WOODS

Enjoy delightfully illustrated characters
in this playful romp among the trees.
Learn a little about nature and get
a few surprises as day turns to night.

Dragons Love Farts: They're More Fun Than Tacos!
Published by Tinker & Swag, Henderson, NV
www.tinkerandswag.com
Author: Hollywood Kay
Illustrator: Yorris Handoko
Copyright©2022

Paperback ISBN: 978-1-951696-07-8
Library of Congress Control Number: 2021948565
First Edition
Printed in the U.S.A.

STEM.ORG
REVIEWED
EDUCATIONAL MEDIA

STEM.ORG
AUTHENTICATED
EDUCATIONAL PRODUCT

A limited supply of our STEM.org
reviewed and authenticated hardcover
is launching exclusively thru Tinker & Swag.
Kids can naturally learn about features in SPACE
while having fun and enjoying the story.
To receive an alert, please sign up at
www.tinkerandswag.com

Tinker & SWAG

Dragons

Love

Farts

They're More Fun Than Tacos!

Hollywood Kay

Yorris Handoko

Oh how scary a dragon can be
when blowing its flames straight out at me!
But sure as a rocket flies higher and higher,
there's something much worse than a dragon's hot fire.

You'll hold your breath till your face turns to blue
when dragons are farting all around you.
If you get a dragon for riding or viewing,
all of those farts will be your undoing.

Dragons are farting all over the world,
there is no escape when their gasses are hurled.
You're minding your business but it doesn't matter,
dragons will fart just to laugh as you scatter.

BOOM!

Some dragons once tried to bury these troubles
by farting in caves to trap the big bubbles.
But farts underground were truly 'No Bueno!'
They quickly became an exploding volcano.

A jolly old dragon who used to eat greens,
once stumbled upon a bucket of beans.
He gobbled them quick, without hesitation.
Now the 'Farting Parade' has his reservation.

Read on and explore this farting bonanza,
it's tasteless— but funny; an *extravaganza!*
Some dragons are silly, a real giggly bunch,
they'll bounce as they fart just to ruin your lunch!

Big bellied dragons who love to eat cheese,
blow out a funk that stinks up the breeze.
They'll even put holes in our atmosphere
as they fart among cows year after year.

They fart when they run or fly like a bird.
Now hush; uh-oh, what's that I just heard?
Yikes! Pinch your nose, run fast as you can;
a dragon just farted behind that old van!

Hot jalapeños were this dragon's desire.
But that spice turned his farts into hot pepper fire.

It caused so much chaos as he jittered about
that he sat in the pond 'till those peppers came out.

FWOOMP!

A dragon once landed on a pirate ship's deck.
Then let out a fart after causing the wreck.

It rousted the Captain right out of his bunk
and that's when the dragon blamed their pet skunk!

Don't expect to be rescued from ivory towers
when dragons have claimed you with funky fart powers.
This damsel believed that knight was the one.
But look how a fart made him turn tail and run!

Did you honestly think this book would be boring
when tooting's more fun than a dragon who's snoring?

Now get to bed, before dragons start farting;
'cuz they're loud just like tubas all stopping and starting.

Think about sheep and start counting their number
so dragons won't fart and ruin your slumber.
Cuddle up quick as you rest your sweet head
and dream of Estrella, who farts rainbows instead.

Made in the USA
Middletown, DE
10 January 2024

47616389R00018